The Flow Zone

How to Maximize Productivity and Joy

Freudian Trips

Copyright Page

Published by Omniterra Media Inc

First Edition

Visit the author's website at www.freudiantrips.com

Disclaimer

The views and opinions expressed in this book are those of the author(s) and do not necessarily reflect the official policy or position of any other agency, organization, employer, or company. The contents of this book are for informational and educational purposes only and are not intended to serve as professional advice, diagnosis, or treatment.

The information provided in this book is believed to be accurate and reliable as of the date of publication. However, it may include some errors or inaccuracies, and no warranty or guarantee is provided regarding the accuracy, timeliness, or applicability of the content.

Readers are encouraged to consult with professional philosophers, educators, or other qualified professionals where appropriate for personalized advice. The author(s) and publisher shall not be liable for any loss, damage, or harm caused or alleged to be caused, directly or indirectly, by the information or ideas contained, suggested, or referenced in this book.

By reading this book, the reader acknowledges and agrees that they are solely responsible for how they interpret and apply the information contained herein.

This book may also include references to other works, studies, and sources. These references are provided for further reading and exploration and do not imply endorsement or validation of the specific theories, viewpoints, or interpretations presented in those works.

Introduction: Unlocking the Power of Flow

Have you ever been so absorbed in an activity that you lost track of time? Hours melt away, the outside world fades into the background, and you feel energized and focused like never before. That's a taste of what psychologists call "flow." It's a state of optimal experience where we feel our best and perform our best – a key ingredient of a fulfilling life.

Think of flow like being swept away by a powerful current in a river. You're not struggling against the water, nor are you drifting aimlessly. You're moving effortlessly with the flow, completely present and in the zone.

But flow isn't magic. Our brains are wired for it! When we're in flow, certain chemicals like dopamine (our reward chemical) get a boost. This creates a feeling of pleasure and motivation that keeps us hooked on the task at hand. At the same time, brain regions associated with self-consciousness and worry temporarily quiet down.

Why does flow matter? Imagine always bringing your A-game to whatever you do. Work becomes less like a chore and more like a fun challenge. Learning is easier, creativity soars, and everyday life feels richer. Flow helps us tap into our hidden potential, leading to growth, increased confidence, and a deep sense of joy along the way.

My Flow Story

I've always been a bit of a tinkerer. As a kid, I could get lost for hours taking apart old radios or building forts in the woods. That sense of time disappearing, of just being totally immersed, was always the best part. It wasn't until years later that I learned there was a name for this feeling—flow. Now, whether I'm writing, playing music, or even tackling a challenging workout, I actively try to unlock that flow state, knowing it's the sweet spot where I truly thrive.

You have flow experiences too, even if you haven't labeled them yet. Think back to times of effortless focus and enjoyment—maybe while playing a sport, making art, or having a deep conversation. Those were likely moments of flow. Understanding this powerful state can help you make more of them happen.

Chapter 1: Decoding Flow

What Exactly IS Flow?

Imagine you're playing a video game. It's tough but not impossible, and you're totally into it. You're reacting quickly, making smart calls, and the points are racking up. Time flies, worries disappear, and you feel a satisfying sense of accomplishment. That, in a nutshell, is flow.

Flow has a few defining features:

- **Deep Focus:** Your attention is locked on the task like a laser beam. It's the opposite of that scattered, can't-concentrate feeling.
- **Sense of Control:** You feel like you're in the driver's seat, even if the challenge is pretty hard.
- **Joy in the Doing:** The activity itself is fun or deeply satisfying, instead of just being a means to an end.
- **Distorted Time:** Hours can feel like minutes, or vice versa!

Your Brain on Flow

Flow isn't just a feeling – it's changes happening in your brain! Think of it like your brain's "happy place." Here's a simplified look:

- **The Reward Boost:** Dopamine, a brain chemical linked to pleasure and motivation, gets released. This makes the activity feel extra good, keeping you going.
- **Less Inner Critic:** Brain areas related to self-judgment take a break. So you're less worried about messing up, which frees you up to take those creative risks.

The Psychology of Flow

There are a few mental ingredients necessary for flow to happen:

- **Focused Attention:** No multitasking here! Flow thrives on single-minded concentration.
- **Feeling in Charge:** You need to believe your actions have an impact, even if the task itself is difficult.
- **Instant Feedback:** Knowing how you're doing as you go along is key. Think of a game's score, or how a painting visibly changes with each brushstroke.
- **Doing It for the Love:** The activity needs to be rewarding in itself. If you're only doing it for an external reward (money, praise), true flow is less likely.

Flow is a powerful state, but it doesn't mean things become magically easy. True flow usually involves

stretching yourself and putting in some serious mental effort!

Chapter 2: Where the Flow Grows

You might picture flow as something reserved for elite athletes or artists in the zone. But the truth is flow can happen anywhere, to anyone! Let's explore where this amazing state tends to pop up.

Flow Hotspots

- **Sports:** The classic example! Think of a basketball player lost in the rhythm of the game, a runner finding that perfect stride, or a rock climber navigating a tricky route with laser focus.
- **Music:** Whether you're playing an instrument, singing your heart out, or just deeply absorbed in a moving piece of music, those moments of pure connection are often flow in action.
- **Creative Work:** The deep satisfaction of writing, painting, coding, or building something feels amazing. That's when flow often sneaks in, bringing ideas to life.

- **Learning:** Totally engrossed in a good book? Tackling a tricky puzzle? When learning feels enjoyable and challenging, flow is likely near!
- **Work:** Yes, even work! A satisfying project, a problem you're determined to solve – these can bring unexpected flow moments.

Flow Goes Everywhere

Flow isn't limited to specific hobbies or jobs. Here's how it shows up in different areas of life:

- **Flow with People:** Deep conversations where you lose track of time, playing with kids where imagination takes over – these can be surprisingly flowy.
- **Flow in Nature:** The peace of a hike, the awe of a beautiful view, the simple act of gardening can bring that feeling of being effortlessly present.
- **Flow in Helping Others:** Acts of service, whether volunteering or just small kindnesses, can produce a unique sense of purpose and absorption.

Everyday Flow

Can you get that flow feeling while doing dishes or commuting? Absolutely! It's not always about grand activities. Here's how to find flow in the ordinary:

- **Turn Chores into Challenges:** Set a timer and see how much laundry you can fold before it beeps. Make cleaning the bathroom feel like a speed challenge with upbeat music.

- **Mindful Moments:** Even a short break can become flow-like. Focus fully on the taste of your coffee, the feeling of the sun on your skin – be completely present.
- **Micro-Flow at Work:** Can you find flow in a specific task like writing a report or organizing data? Block out distractions and just dive into that one thing.

The key is to look for those pockets of absorption, joy in the process, and that sense of time slipping away, wherever they happen!

Chapter 3: Setting the Stage for Flow

Think of flow like Goldilocks and the porridge: It needs things to be 'just right'. The ease of the task renders it monotonous. Too hard, and you get overwhelmed or frustrated. Flow thrives in that magical middle ground.

The Skill-Challenge Balance

Imagine a tightrope walker. If the rope's on the ground, it's no sweat, but also no fun. If the rope's too high, the fear takes over. The thrilling flow state is somewhere in between—a high wire, but one you feel with practice you could master.

The same applies to all sorts of activities! You need:

- **A Stretch, Not a Snap:** The task should push you a little beyond your current abilities–you need to learn or grow in some way.
- **Belief in Yourself:** Even if it's tough, you need to think, "I can do this, with effort." That keeps you from giving up before the flow kicks in.

Clear Goals & Feedback

Think of trying to navigate in a thick fog. Flow hates that! Here's why goals and feedback matter:

- **Know Where You're Going:** What exactly are you trying to achieve? A clear goal keeps you from drifting aimlessly, whether it's finishing a painting or solving a work problem.
- **Checkpoints Along the Way:** How do you know if you're making progress? That "progress feeling" feeds on feedback – a score in a game, a rough draft coming together, a customer smiling after you help them.

Your Flow-Friendly Environment

The wrong environment can squash flow before it starts! Here's how to set up your space:

- **Distraction-Free Zone:** Silence your phone, close extra tabs on your computer... protect your concentration like it's precious.
- **Tools at the Ready:** Everything you need should be easily accessible to keep your focus from breaking.
- **Your Feel-Good Space:** Whether it's cozy and quiet or bright and energetic, make sure the atmosphere helps you get in the zone.

The Joy of "Autotelic"

This sounds fancy, but it's simple! It means an activity is its own reward. You're not doing it for money, praise, or external goals—you just love the process itself. Think of a kid lost in play or a hobbyist who forgets to eat because they're so into their project. That's autotelic.

Finding more activities that feel this way increases your chance of experiencing flow.

Remember, flow isn't guaranteed, even if you set things up perfectly. But understanding these conditions puts you in the best position for catching that elusive and amazing flow state!

Chapter 4: When Flow Gets Stuck

Even when you're chasing flow with the best intentions, things can get in the way. Let's face those flow blockers head-on, so you can break free and get back to that awesome focused feeling.

Inside Job: Mental Roadblocks

Sometimes the biggest flow-stoppers are in our own heads! Here are a few common culprits:

- **The Inner Critic:** That nagging voice saying "You're not good enough" or "This is going to be a disaster." It can sap your confidence before you even begin.
- **Fear of Failure:** Being so worried about messing up that you freeze, holding back from the task.
- **Perfectionist Trap:** Demanding absolute perfection from yourself can lead to a constant feeling of never being good enough, which kills flow's joyful spirit.

- **Procrastination Station:** Putting things off makes tasks feel bigger and scarier in our minds, making flow way harder to reach.

The World Gets in the Way: External Obstacles

The environment around you plays a role too. These flow-blockers can pop up:

- **Distraction Attack:** The constant buzz of notifications, chatty coworkers, or a messy workspace fracture your attention and make deep focus impossible.
- **Not Enough Fuel:** Trying to flow when you're exhausted, hungry, or just feeling physically unwell is an uphill battle.
- **Missing Pieces:** Not having the right tools, resources, or information can make a task feel frustratingly out of reach instead of a satisfying challenge.

Flow Rescue Mission: Strategies to Overcome

Don't worry, there are solutions! Try these approaches to break through the barriers:

- **Mindfulness Check-In:** Simply noticing your thoughts and feelings without judgment can help. Just say to yourself, "Okay, I'm feeling nervous," or "My mind is wandering." This breaks their control over you a little.
- **Reframe It:** Instead of, "I'll never get this," tell yourself, "This is challenging, and I'm going to learn."

- **Boundaries Are Beautiful:** Let others know when you need focus time. Turn off notifications. Claim a quiet space. Protect your flow!
- **Break it Down:** Big tasks feel overwhelming. Start with the smallest step, just to get moving. It often makes the rest feel less daunting.

Remember, overcoming obstacles is part of the journey to finding more flow. With awareness and practice, you'll get better at navigating the barriers and getting back into your zone!

Chapter 5: Your Flow Training Plan

Think of cultivating flow like building a muscle. It takes consistent effort and the right approach. This chapter is your training guide for making flow a bigger part of your life!

Flow-Booster #1: Deep Practice

This isn't about mindlessly repeating something. Deep practice is all about focused, intentional effort:

- **Break It Down:** Focus on mastering one small part of the skill at a time. Trying to tackle too much at once overwhelms your brain.
- **Challenge = Growth:** Keep pushing yourself slightly beyond your current level.
- **Seek Feedback:** This could be a teacher, a coach, or just being honest with yourself about how things are going. Feedback keeps you on track.

Flow-Booster #2: Smart Goals

Having clear goals is essential, but the specifics matter for maximum flow:

- **Just-Right Difficulty:** Remember that Goldilocks sweet spot? Goals should stretch you but feel achievable.
- **Break It Down:** Big goals can be overwhelming. Smaller sub-goals create those satisfying 'checkpoints' that keep you motivated.
- **Make Them Meaningful:** Goals connected to your values or things you care deeply about will naturally be more engaging.

Flow-Booster #3: Master Your Focus

Training your attention is like training for a marathon:

- **Start Small:** Set a timer and try to focus on a single task for 5 minutes, then gradually increase.
- **Anchor Yourself:** Use your breath as an anchor when your mind wanders. Just gently bring your attention back to the feeling of each inhale and exhale.
- **Environment Counts:** Pick a time and place where you're least likely to be disturbed to give your focus a fighting chance.

Mindfulness: Your Flow Superpower

Being fully present in the here and now is like giving flow a VIP pass. Here's how:

- **Notice Without Judgment:** Observe your thoughts and feelings as they pass through your mind, like watching clouds in the sky. Don't get hooked on them, just let them drift by.

- **Senses Are Your Friends:** Tune into the sights, sounds, smells, and physical sensations you usually ignore. This brings you back to the present.

The Flow Mindset

It's not just about *what* you do, but *how* you approach it:

- **Embrace the Challenge:** See difficulties as exciting opportunities for growth instead of frustrating roadblocks.
- **Kindness to Yourself:** Mistakes are part of learning! Instead of beating yourself up, ask "What can I learn from this?"
- **Celebrate Progress:** Notice even small steps forward. This helps combat that perfectionist voice and keeps the motivation flowing (pun intended!)

Design Your Flow Life

Small shifts can have a big impact:

- **Audit Your Time:** Where do you experience flow? Can you do more of those activities? What drains you and could be minimized?
- **Tiny Flow Moments:** Infuse everyday tasks with focus. Really pay attention to that coffee you make or your walk to work.
- **Rest & Recharge:** Flow is way less likely to happen if you're running on empty. Taking breaks is essential!

This journey is ongoing! Be patient, keep experimenting, and celebrate as flow becomes a more frequent visitor in your life.

Chapter 6: The Amazing Payoffs of Flow

Imagine a life where work feels more like play, learning is enjoyable, and you have a deeper sense of satisfaction day-to-day. That's the potential power of flow! Let's dive into the incredible benefits it offers.

Flow = Performance Booster

When you're in flow, amazing things happen:

- **Laser Focus:** Distractions fade away, and you become super-efficient. You get more done in less time!
- **Peak Performance:** Whether playing sports, giving presentations, or tackling complex work problems, flow lets you tap into your best abilities.
- **The Joy of Work:** Even tasks you don't normally love become more engaging in flow, making work way less of a drag.

Happiness Upgrade

Flow isn't just about achievement; it changes how you *feel*:

- **Positivity Boost:** Flow releases feel-good chemicals in your brain, creating a natural high.
- **Less Worry & Stress:** That inner critic quiets down, giving you a break from overthinking and self-doubt.
- **Deep Satisfaction:** Achieving things through your own effort cultivates true contentment—much more fulfilling than fleeting external pleasures.

Finding Your Why: Purpose & Meaning

When you're frequently absorbed in flow experiences, life feels richer. You discover:

- **Connection to Something Bigger:** Flow can take you outside yourself, feeling a part of something greater—whether it's nature, a creative project, or contributing to your community.
- **Your Unique Strengths:** Flow shows where you shine, building confidence in your talents and your place in the world.

Mental Superpowers: Learning, Creativity, Problem-Solving

Flow transforms how your brain works:

- **Learning Accelerator:** You pick up new skills and information more easily when you're fully engaged and enjoying the process.

- **Creativity Unleashed:** With the fear and self-judgment out of the way, flow gives your imagination the freedom to soar.
- **Problem-Solving Ninja:** In a flow state, you see new connections and solutions more easily.

The Path to Your Best Self

Psychologists talk about "self-actualization," which is basically becoming the most fulfilled version of yourself. Flow is a powerful tool on this journey because it helps you:

- **Overcome Obstacles:** Flow shows you what you're truly capable of, building belief in yourself.
- **Growth Zone = Comfort Zone:** The flow state trains you to enjoy challenges and keep pushing your potential.
- **Live in the Moment:** Flow teaches you to find joy in the present instead of always chasing the future or dwelling on the past.

Important Note: Flow is awesome, but it's not the key to happiness 24/7 (nor should it be!). Life has ups and downs. But having flow as a regular visitor makes navigating the challenges easier and the good times even sweeter.

Chapter 7: Where You'll Find Flow (Spoiler: Everywhere!)

Flow isn't limited to elite athletes or artists. Let's explore real-world examples of this amazing state in action and how it can transform different aspects of our lives.

Flow All-Stars: Case Studies

- **The Athlete:** Think of a gymnast completely in the zone, nailing a complex routine, or a runner finding that perfect rhythm where the miles melt away.
- **The Artist:** A musician lost in the music, a writer so immersed in the story that the world fades away, or a painter seeing the finished piece in their mind's eye and making it real.
- **The Professional:** A surgeon fully absorbed in a delicate procedure, a coder finding elegant solutions to a problem, or a teacher captivated by the spark in their students' eyes.
- **Everyday Heroes:** The home cook completely focused on perfecting a recipe, the gardener

engrossed in tending to their plants, or the devoted volunteer finding their groove.

Flow School: Learning Reimagined

Imagine classrooms where kids are excited to learn, not just going through the motions. Here's how flow fits in:

- **Hands-On Projects:** Learning by doing (making, building, experimenting) is naturally more engaging.
- **Choice & Challenge:** Kids take some ownership over their learning, with tasks matched to their skill levels.
- **"Playful" Learning:** Elements of games, healthy competition, and creative exploration can make acquiring knowledge more fun.

The Flow-Forward Workplace

Work can be a major source of flow... or a major flow blocker! Here's how to boost flow on the job:

- **Match Tasks to Skills:** That 'sweet spot' applies here too. Boredom and burnout happen on both ends.
- **Autonomy & Trust:** People do their best work with some control over *how* they get things done.
- **Clear Goals & Feedback:** Knowing what you're aiming for (and how you're doing) is essential for flow.

Flow & the Spirit

For many, flow feels connected to something deeper than the task itself. Here are some ways that connection shows up:

- **Awe & Wonder:** Nature's beauty, profound music, or acts of compassion can bring a flow-like state of absorption and transcending the everyday self.
- **Meditation & Mindfulness:** Stilling the mind can open the door to a flow-like sense of peace and presence.
- **Service to Others:** Losing yourself in helping others can tap into a sense of purpose and connectedness beyond yourself.

Important to Note: You don't have to be religious to experience this aspect of flow. It's more about finding a deep sense of something beyond your immediate concerns.

Flow is a powerful force for good on both the individual and collective level. The more we understand and cultivate it, the better equipped we are to create a more fulfilling world, both for ourselves and others.

Conclusion: Flow – Your Invitation to a Fuller Life

Throughout this journey, we've unpacked the science of flow, explored where it shows up, faced down its obstacles, and discovered the incredible benefits it offers. It's time to bring it all together into the big picture.

Key Takeaways

- **Flow Is Natural:** You've tasted flow, even if it was fleeting. Our brains are wired for it!
- **Flow Is Trainable:** With the right mindset and strategies, you can create more flow experiences in all areas of your life.
- **Flow Matters:** It's not just about feeling good in the moment (though that's awesome!), but about developing skills, becoming your best self, and finding a deep sense of fulfillment.

Flow: The Transformation Tool

Think of flow as a key that unlocks something amazing within you. It helps you:

- **Break Through Limits:** Experience what you're truly capable of – physically, mentally, and creatively.
- **Live More Fully:** Become fully absorbed in the present instead of fretting about the past or future.
- **Tap Into Joy & Meaning:** Discover satisfaction beyond external pleasures, building a life that feels deeply authentic.

The Future of Flow

The journey continues! Here are exciting possibilities:

- **Research:** More is yet to be discovered about how flow works in the brain and how to best promote it.
- **Applications:** Imagine flow-centered approaches to education, therapy, workplace design, and social change.
- **Unleashing Potential:** As flow becomes more accessible to everyone, it could transform society, fostering greater well-being, innovation, and connection.

Your Invitation

This book is only the beginning of your flow journey. Notice when flow arises, no matter how briefly it lasts. Use the strategies you've learned and keep experimenting. You'll be amazed at how much richer and more enjoyable life becomes when flow is a frequent guest.

Remember, flow is within reach. All you have to do is start paying attention, make small adjustments, and embrace the process. May you live a life filled with focus, joy, and the deep satisfaction that comes from tapping into your true potential.

About Freudian Trips

Welcome to Freudian Trips, your dedicated platform for diving deep into the world of psychology. We are more than just a YouTube channel or a book publisher. We are a beacon of enlightenment, making complex psychological concepts accessible and engaging for all.

Our YouTube channel is a rich repository of psychology made simple. We take the profound and often complex ideas from the world of psychology and break them down into digestible, easy-to-understand content. From the foundational theories of Freud to the cognitive insights of Piaget, we cover a broad spectrum of psychological schools and thoughts, making psychology accessible to everyone, regardless of their background or prior knowledge.

As a book publisher, we take the same approach, transforming intricate psychological theories into comprehensible narratives. Our books are not just collections of words, but vessels of wisdom that make psychology approachable and relatable. We believe that psychology should not be confined to academic circles, but should be available to all who seek to understand the human mind and behavior.

At Freudian Trips, we believe in the power of curiosity and the pursuit of knowledge. We are here to stoke the fires of your curiosity, to guide you on your intellectual journey, and to help you navigate the fascinating world of psychology.

If you are someone who is not afraid to question, to explore, and to learn, then you are in the right place. Join us on this journey of exploration, as we make psychology easy to understand, one concept at a time.

Be sure to visit our Youtube channel at:
www.freudiantrips.com/youtube

You can also visit us on the web at www.freudiantrips.com

Welcome to The Freudian Trip community. Stay curious. Stay enlightened.